# Closing The Doors

## What To Do After Being Delivered!

WEST PALM BEACH

FL, 33407

# DAVID GRANT

Copyright © 2023 David GRANT

All rights reserved.

No part of this publication may be reproduced, copied, stored in a retrieval system, transmitted, scanned in any form, or under any conditions, including, photocopying, electronic, recording, or otherwise, without the author's written permission, David Grant.

ISBN: 978-1-954755-81-9

Published by:
Restoration of the Breach without Borders
West Palm Beach, Florida 33407
restorativeauthor@gmail.com
Tele: (475) 233 9008

Book cover design by:
Angus Designs
(876)-809-1743

# TABLE OF CONTENTS

| | |
|---|---|
| Dedication | 5 |
| Endorsements | 6 |
| Acknowledgments | 10 |
| Foreword | 12 |
| Closing the Doors | 15 |
| Introduction | 15 |
| Chapter One: Close The Door, Please! | |
| What Are The Doors? | 1 |
| Chapter 2: Letting Darkness In. | |
| How are doors Opened? | 11 |
| Chapter 3: I Do Not Want This! | |
| What can/Will Enter? | 25 |
| Chapter 4: Oops! There Is A Door Here! | |
| Are There Doors At Church? | 28 |
| Chapter 5: The Devil In Your Space | |
| How Could He Be? | 35 |

Chapter 6: Breaking The Chains

Can I Truly Be Free?                                46

Chapter 7: Give Me Those Keys!

Keys Grant Or Deny Access                           55

Chapter 8: Agree With Your Adversary

How Important Is This?                              63

Chapter 9: Break Down That Altar                    70

Chapter 10: Free At Last

How Do I Keep My Freedom?                           79

Chapter 11: Moving On

How Can I Stay Free?                                87

Closing Words                                       92

Testimonies                                         94

About the Author                                    104

# DEDICATION

I dedicate this book to my spiritual father, Apostle Dr. V.T. Williams, the man God used to preach me out of sin's darkness into the marvelous light of the Kingdom of God.

Sir, you have taught me how to love the Lord God with all my heart and serve Him with my entire existence. Also, to have a passion for God's presence and compassion for His people.

I have had the privilege of working alongside you in many different scenarios. I have seen your passion for God, and I have seen you lead many souls to Christ. Numerous Miracles have been wroth through your faith in God, and I endeavor to emulate you. Thanks for your shining example of what it means to be a man of God.

"Pops," I love you.
Thank you!!

# ENDORSEMENTS

*"Closing The Doors"* is an excellent resource to help those who have received deliverance from demonic influences/possession. This book provides practical steps and prayers to assist in maintaining one's deliverance. Too many who were delivered find themselves in a cycle of being delivered from one thing, and yet, under the influence again of more and even stronger spirits. Often, this results from ignorance concerning how to maintain their deliverance – "keeping the doors open".

Pastor David Grant is an "astute" deliverance minister who possesses a keen gift of discernment. He is powerfully anointed to set the captives free. For over 40 years, he has functioned effectively to bring deliverance to so many who have been held in bondage through generational curses, witchcraft, wilful and/or ignorant acts, etc., which has opened doors in their lives to the domination of Satan and the forces/beings of the kingdom of darkness.

I highly recommend this book as a resource for all who are in deliverance ministry as it will assist the people whom they have helped to maintain their deliverance. I further recommend to all who have been recipients of deliverance having been set free by the power of God. However, this book will also release knowledge and understanding to all who read it as the information is invaluable. All praise to the Lord for using His servant David Grant to continue the mission of destroying the works of the devil and the kingdom of darkness.

-Apostle Dr. Althea M. Grant
His Abiding Presence Evangelistic Ministries, Inc.
Port Chester, New York

******

I have known David for over 10 years and this book epitomizes the man, his love for God, and his unwavering desire to see people in general set free. I have also read many spiritual warfare books. However, there are a number of things significant about this book that I absolutely love. The numerous personal experiences serve to open the eyes, minds, and spirits of many. The countless references to scripture set this book apart from others and provide validity. The ease of transition from chapter to chapter provides a clear outline of what takes place within us as well as how to identify the issue, denounce the connections, and break the chains. Needless to say, this spiritual warfare book is a staple for every Christian desiring to live victoriously.

-Apostle E. G. McLean
Overseer
Kingdom Builders Worship Centre
International Ministries

******

In his enlightening book, Pastor David Grant unveils the hidden workings of darkness, shedding light on the reality of the adversary, Satan, and his legion of demons. This essential read is plain, practical, and pertinent to the challenges of our modern era. Every believer should seize the opportunity to gain insight into the adversary's agenda by acquiring a copy.

-Oscar A. Green
Author of The Jesus Magic

******

*"Closing The Doors"* by Rev. David C. Grant is indeed a very timely, profound, but very simple book about a subject that attracts so much attention in the body of Christ.

This is a one-sitting read filled with such powerful scriptural insight. As I read, I heard your voice, your passion for the body of Christ to live victorious, come out in each chapter.

This book led me to pray the prayers and check myself to see if there were any open doors in my life.

Congratulations and thank you my friend and partner in ministry.

-Rev. Dr. Kirk Campbell
Pastor
Maranatha Ministries International Westmoreland, President of Prayer 2000 Ministries

# ACKNOWLEDGMENTS

Thanks to God for calling me into this ministry; through His power and grace, I have been delivered to become a deliverer.

Thanks to my wife, Juliet, and our children for their support throughout the years, the late nights, and sometimes absence from a few special events.

Special mention of three ministers who are now in glory with whom I have had the privilege to work: Dwight Thompson, Bishop Joseph Ade-Gold, and Rev. Lloyd Maxwell.

The Reverends Errol Hall and Kirk Campbell are men with an unwavering passion for seeing the kingdom of Satan brought to naught. We have worked tirelessly in bringing deliverance to so many over these years.

Dr. Donald Karl Stewart, to whom I owe an outstanding gratitude for teaching and equipping me by giving me approximately 100 books from his vast library when he was migrating to Zambia. Eternally grateful to you, sir. Special acknowledgments must be extended to

Bishop O'mar Wedderburn. And Rudolphe Neath for their contribution as editors.

To the hundreds of people who trusted God in me even when I was sixteen and inexperienced. I pray that all have maintained their deliverance, and if not, here is a new resource that can help in that effort.

To God be the God!

# FOREWORD

"Uncle David, I need deliverance!" These are some of the words I remember uttering many years ago. This was met with the response, "Don't we all need deliverance?"

It is with great enthusiasm and admiration that I write this foreword for *"Closing the Doors: What to Do After You Have Been Delivered!"* A book authored by my mentor and friend, David Grant (Uncle David). As someone who has had the privilege of knowing David, working alongside him in ministry, and witnessing first-hand the transformative impact of his work, I am thrilled to see his insights and wisdom captured within these pages.

David Grant is not just an author, pastor, and counselor; he is an inspiration of hope and guidance for those who have journeyed through the challenging and often tumultuous path of emancipation and maintenance from demonic forces and influences. His personal growth, resilience, and freedom are a testament to his profound knowledge and understanding of the spirit realm, its activities, and what it means to confront the kingdom of darkness and emerge victorious.

*"Closing the Doors"* delves into a crucial and often unexplored terrain of personal transformation. It addresses the period that follows deliverance, a phase that many might overlook in their pursuit of change and healing. David offers a compassionate and insightful roadmap for those who have taken the courageous step of closing the doors of their past and embarking on a new chapter of life. Within these pages, readers will encounter a treasured trove of wisdom, practical advice, and stories of real-life individuals who have faced adversity and emerged stronger on the other side. David's writing is saturated with empathy, understanding, and the deepest, profound respect for each individual or family affected. His words serve as a reminder that even after we have been delivered from our past struggles, the journey of healing and growth is an ongoing, transformative process.

*"Closing the Doors"* is more than a book; it is a lifeline for those who have embarked on the path of personal growth and change. David's insights provide a

reassuring and knowledgeable presence, guiding readers through the intricacies of managing newfound freedom and embracing a life that is truly their own. As you open the pages of this book, I encourage you to do so with an open heart and a willingness to learn from a mentor who has walked the path and is now generously sharing his wisdom. In these words, you will find the strength to continue your journey of emancipation, resilience, growth, and empowerment.

I extend my gratitude to David Grant for his unwavering commitment to helping others and for writing a book that will undoubtedly make a profound difference in the lives of those who seek healing and transformation. *"Closing the Doors"* is a testament that true freedom from demonic possession, oppression, and influences is available for all who dare to pursue it.

With admiration and appreciation,
Mentee

-Rev. Leostone Morrison
Author: Mind Renewal: Biblical
Secrets To A Better You

# CLOSING THE DOORS INTRODUCTION

**F**or centuries, the authors of many novels and the keyboards of many movie writers have scripted the stories of this unseen war that has been ensuing between the forces of good and evil. We are taught to believe that darkness and light cannot coexist, so there is a constant battle between them for supremacy.

Aligning with a Christian worldview, the Bible is our ultimate knowledge source. Paul writes in 2 Corinthians 10:4 that we are in a war that is not carnal but spiritual, and the weapons are not carnal armament. He goes even further in Ephesians 6:10-20 to identify who we are fighting against, the weapons, and how to use them to gain victory.

The war between God and the devil is one for our worship and souls. Each has an army with a hierarchical system, and both lead a host of supernatural beings. For God, it is His holy angels; for the devil, it is demons.

There have been many misconceptions concerning demons, their existence, capabilities, and destiny. Two common ones are:

- ✓ Demons do not exist; if they do, they just dwell in the atmosphere and have nothing to do with daily evil.
- ✓ Demons cannot possess humans but can only disrupt human lives.

The Bible addresses these misconceptions (read Mark 5:1-20; Matt. 8:28-34; Luke 8:26-39; 13:10-17; 4:31-37 & Acts 16:16).

Yet, even with proof from the word of God, many have reclined that they are powerless against these evil spirits.

I recall a story of a preacher who had an encounter–a visitation from Jesus that transformed his thinking and, subsequently, his life. Once, while talking to Jesus, a demon in the form of a monkey came between Jesus and himself to interrupt their conversation. Consequently, the preacher could no longer hear what Jesus was saying. The preacher perplexingly asked, *"Why don't you send this demon away?" Jesus replied, "That is not my responsibility but yours, for I have given you authority." "Behold, I give unto you the power to tread on serpents and scorpions, and over all the power of the enemy: and nothing shall by any means hurt you". (Luke 10:19)*

After being reminded of the power given to him, the preacher used his God-given authority to rebuke the demon/evil spirit, which disappeared, and he could hear Jesus again. The preacher allowed the demon to interrupt his interaction with Jesus because of his ignorance. However, after he received the revelation, he knew what to do. *"My people are destroyed for lack of knowledge: because they have rejected knowledge, I will also reject thee, that thou shalt be no priest to me: seeing thou has forgotten the law of thy God, I will also forget thy children". (Hosea 4:6)*

Are the days of ignorance and misconceptions ending? In this information and technological age, it requires more energy to be uninformed than enlightened - ignorance is in no way an excuse. This illumination has brought about what some have regarded as the rebirth of the deliverance ministry. Honestly, the ministry never died.

Several believers see deliverance as a call for only exceptional individuals (an excuse they propose because they are fearful). Some see deliverance as something that must be done. Others think of the ministry as the means to gain popularity and showboating of spiritual prowess - a 'Ghost Buster' mentality.

Remember the scripture: *"When a defiling evil spirit is expelled from someone, it drifts through the desert looking for an oasis, some unsuspecting soul it can bedevil. When it does not find anyone, it says, 'I'll go back to my old haunt.' On return, it finds the person spotlessly clean but vacant. It then runs out and rounds up seven other spirits eviler than itself, and they all move in, whooping it up. That person ends up far worse off than if he'd never gotten cleaned up in the first place". (Mat 12:43 -45 Message)* Sadly, many who administer deliverance are more preoccupied with their victory over the demons/evil spirits than educating the candidates on staying free. Deliverance ministers must consider the well-being of the lives they 'deliver' to be their top priority–not their popularity.

However, thankfully, some ministers legitimately see the ministry for what it is-a part of the Great Impartation: "These are some of the signs that will accompany believers: They will throw out demons in my name, they will speak in new tongues, they will take snakes in their hands, they will drink poison and not be hurt, and they will lay hands on the sick and make them well" (Mar 16:17 & 18 Message).

## *Where do demons come from?*

This age-old question is always full of diverse responses. There are at least three schools of thought known to me at this point:

1. They are the souls of the dead from an alleged pre-Adamic race that died in the first flood that supposedly took place between Genesis 1:1 and Genesis 1:2.

2. They are the souls of the offspring of the "sons of God" and the "daughters of men" mentioned in Genesis 6.
3. They are the fallen angels who rebelled against God with Lucifer, according to Revelation 12:9.

Whatever the schools of thought one subscribes to, all schools agree to the existence of demons. This book aims not to give a theological treatise on the origin and reality of demons but to help people who have encountered them maintain their deliverance by closing their doors.

# CHAPTER ONE
# CLOSE THE DOOR, PLEASE!
## *What Are The Doors?*

A door or doorway is an access point of exit or entry. The Living Webster's Encyclopaedic Dictionary of the English Language defines a door as an opening or passage into a room, house, or building, a means of approach or access.

The doorway of demonic access to people's lives is through the ears, eyes, emotions, etc. The critical points of entry are the ears, eyes, and mouth. Do you remember that Sunday/Sabbath school song about watching your eyes, ears, lips, hands, and feet, for there is a Father up above looking down in tender love, watch your eyes, ears, lips, hands, and feet? The indication proposes that what you see, hear, speak, and do can affect your outcome. You must guard these entry points against demonic influence and intrusion.

Your body is a house; it holds your actual being: your spirit and soul. Your body also accommodates whatever you, or someone else responsible for you, allow entrance, e.g. parents, guardians, and ministers. Sexually molested children are susceptible to the door of anger, suicide, promiscuity, also social and emotional deviation, opening up from the terrible occurrence.

I have had a few deliverance sessions where the demon admitted to being in the person from the womb. How can this be? The state of a mother during pregnancy has a lot to do with a child's characteristics, behavioral patterns, and spiritual condition.

## *Recollection #1*

I recall a young lady who experienced uneasiness during her pregnancy, and the only thing she found soothing was listening to her local gospel radio station. After her son's birth, he, too, was uneasy, and the only thing that calmed him was the same gospel station his mother listened to. Do you think this was a mere coincidence?

## *Recollection #2*

Another mother, during pregnancy, found out her child's father was seeing another woman. She would trail him to the other woman's house, and as soon as he got there and settled down, she would throw stones on the roof of the house and then run away. You may ask, how does this link to the unborn child? It turns out that the child (a girl) grew up and was involved in several relationships (some as far as engagement). Still, none materialized into marriage, primarily due to her mistrust of men. She was over fifty years old and still unmarried when this book was being written.

Some men say they were born gay or effeminate. However, their mothers' ignorance of the spiritual realm may have been the offshoot of their sons' lifestyles. A mother's actions, speeches, and even thoughts toward her child/children in the womb can affect the child's/children's outcome. Here is a scenario to consider. A father and mother are hoping and planning for a girl to be the new addition to the home. They give their unborn child a female name and subsequently address the developing infant by that name. Innocent, right? Not quite so.

Doing so can open a portal for the entry of an effeminate spirit if the child is a boy. Some people think there is nothing wrong with a male acting like a female, but let the Author of life and the Bible, which is the operational manual, decide. *"Know ye not that the unrighteous shall not inherit the kingdom of God? Be not deceived: neither fornicators, nor idolaters, nor adulterers, nor effeminate, nor abusers of themselves with mankind, nor thieves, nor covetous, nor drunkards, nor revellers, nor extortioners, shall inherit the kingdom of God" (1 Corinthians 6:9-10).*

I read a book some years ago concerning the healing of memories. The author, a clinical psychologist, stated in his book, "The Healing of Memories," that a child's memory starts to develop at six months in the mother's womb. He recounted a session with a twenty-two-year-old client suffering rejection, low self-esteem, and suicidal tendencies. In this session, she was under hypnosis when she began crying and saying, "Daddy, do not leave me; you don't even know if I am a boy or a girl." When the hypnosis was over, the client related the story of being in the hospital (three months in her mother's womb) and experiencing her father's death. While I do not advocate for hypnosis, as I believe it could have negative spiritual implications, I found the story interesting from a scientific and spiritual standpoint.

*Recollection #3*

Let me share another interesting account with you. While pastoring in rural Jamaica, I mentioned in a sermon one Sunday that a mother's state during pregnancy could affect a child's attitude, mannerisms, and characteristics. After the service, a church member began reflecting on a situation he knew of in his community, and being inspired by the sermon, he did some research. A young lady who lived in his community was gay and considered to have been born that way.

The church member asked the mother if she desired a male child while pregnant. The parent confirmed that while the child was in the womb, she spoke to and treated it like a boy. Sometime later, a relative revealed that the mother made a pronouncement over the child that "he" would have sex with all the girls in the community. This young woman was 23 years old at the time of the writing of this book and was known to be sexually active but had never had sexual intercourse with a male.

We must be wise with the words we declare in the atmosphere. The Bible states that death and life are in the power of the tongue, and those who love it shall eat the fruit thereof (Proverbs 18:21). The spoken word created the world; therefore, it was voice-activated. Consequently, we must be mindful of our declarations (including the seemingly insignificant) about ourselves and those around us, as we may create an atmosphere that leads to death rather than life.

Having learned this, my wife and I spoke positively about our unborn children, and I would lay hands on her tummy and prophesy over them. Making declarations like: **"You will be leaders"** and **"You will be born again at a tender age."** We can testify that ALL four of our children became Christians and were baptized in water and the Holy Spirit. They have served in leadership throughout their school lives and continue into their careers. If you plan on having a child/children, please invest in them with positive words while they are still in the womb.

The fashion industry is a thriving vocation saturated with persons who have committed themselves to promulgating satanic agendas and his kingdom for profit under the guise of art. The music fraternity also has evil inspirations. We see more artists today revealing their true object of worship. Music can create atmospheres for good or evil. Music is involved in every form of worship-pagan and Christian. Christians know Satan was the former chief musician and a being of beauty in heaven. So, it is not a light matter for him to warp the entertainment industry to his advantage.

*Recollection #4*

In my childhood, there was a radio station that would play instrumentals on a Sunday afternoon.

This music would profoundly affect me, as it always made me sad, even to tears. In my mid-teens, I was crazy in love with a beautiful young lady who lived approximately four miles from my home. Every day at around 3 p.m., that station would play a song entitled "Through the Fire" by the artist Chaka Khan. It spoke to being willing to go through whatever was required to achieve one's objective. It motivated me to prepare and walk that four-mile journey as if it were next door. Once I heard that song, I was compelled to go see her even though her father told me not to return to his house.

While these may not be demonic, they speak to the power of music. So, imagine the music being manipulated and inspired by evil spirits.

As mentioned, one's mouth is another central doorway, but less acknowledged. The world is voice-activated in both the seen and unseen realms. The physically seen world exists as a result of the unseen spiritual world. Elohim, the invisible Creator, spoke this visible realm into being. We, humans, are the creation in the image and likeness of the Creator. One attribute of the Creator is speaking. Creative power is in our words. You have heard these sayings many times, "What you speak, you will get," "Confess it and receive it," "Name it and claim it," etc. They speak to the reality of the power of confessions. Whether these confessions are negative or positive, they can become a reality.

All these physical access points are within our ability to control. A fruit of the Spirit recorded in Galatians 5:23 in the King James version is known as "temperance." Temperance means self-control; with the aid of the Holy Spirit, we can control ourselves. We can dictate what we listen to, speak, or see to a significant degree.

**Prayer Time**

Father God, in the name of your Son, Jesus Christ of Nazareth, I thank you for revealing that there are doorways to my life that evil spirits may have accessed. Please sanctify these entry points, whether these accesses were while I was in the womb or after that.

Today, I ask that these doorways no longer serve as entrance points to my life but become exits for every demon that would have entered me through them. Let them now become the points of expulsion.

Jesus, I confess all sins (ask the Holy Spirit to bring to your memory) I have committed, which may have granted the devil and his demons access. I repent of (name them) and ask you to cleanse me thoroughly from my sins and those of my fore-parents.

I grant you access by giving you total control of these access points. Do convict me of every sin that can potentially reopen doors I seek to keep closed.

Amen!

# CHAPTER 2
# LETTING DARKNESS IN. HOW ARE DOORS OPENED?

You can do only so much regarding the audio and visuals you come across daily in the public sphere. It is improbable that you never see a billboard of a half-naked person and hear the words of a worldly song belting. How it affects you is determined by what you allow access to you. While you can't control what you see and hear, you can filter what you see and hear. Do you entertain lustful thoughts after seeing or hearing something lewd? Do you pretend you saw or heard nothing, acknowledge what you heard or saw, and consciously try not to make it impact you negatively? Do you see it as art or soft pornography? Sometimes, the door is not abruptly opened but subtly opened over time. Be careful of what you entertain.

## Recollection #5

My wife and I once conducted a deliverance session on a young lady who worked at a graphic arts company. One Friday afternoon, while using the computer to create a design, she began seeing symbols on the screen and fell unconscious. She later described the symbols as astrological and satanic. The deliverance session that started at 5 a.m. on Saturday concluded at 7 p.m. the Sunday. No, we did not spend all that time with her. We took a break, prayed over her, sent her home, and she returned on Sunday morning during service time.

After the session, she told us of her introduction to the occult while living in a boarding house as a teenager. One of the girls in the home had a Ouija board, an occult game that works with the spirit of divination, which the girls enjoyed playing with. The activity, which appeared fun during her adolescence, was the subtle opening of a door leading to her becoming demonized.

## Recollection #6

We also participated in a deliverance session with a young lady who would have been labeled bisexual. Alice's (not her real name) mother discarded her at the city dump. A couple found the baby and took her in. Sadly, her "saviours" sexually abused her. Alice told us she did not know what it was like to stop having sex until she was thirteen. Once, while staying over at a friend's house, at about 4 a.m., the friend woke up to find Alice sucking on her breast.

Alice was unaware of what she was doing as she was under the influence of a demon. Someone brought the matter to our attention. My friend and ministry partner, Kirk Campbell, and I administered deliverance to her, and Alice has since been delivered. In Alice's case, the initial doorway was opened by the rejection of her parents, which led to the opening of the other entrance to sexual abuse from the perverted people who raised her.

## *Recollection #7*

Sarah (not her actual name) was eighteen when Kirk and I met her, and she had already been in several sexual relationships. While doing the deliverance session, one of the demons began speaking, uttering how it was not leaving, and that Sarah belonged to it. The demon revealed it had been in the family line from Sarah's grandmother and had been residing in Sarah all her life. Demons, at times, will claim someone's life because their activities are labeled as normal and accepted by the host. Our after-deliverance counselling session revealed that her mother and grandmother were promiscuous.

No wonder the demon had legal rights to this young lady. These kinds of demonic activities are generational curses, and often, families are identified and called by the demonic activity, further solidifying the demon's hold on that family through the power of our words. Sometimes people say, "That's just how we are as a family", not recognizing they could embrace a generational curse.

## *Recollection #8*

One night, my wife and I had an impromptu session that left an indelible impression on me. It taught me the importance of listening to the Spirit of God. A friend had asked us to come and pray at the house she had just moved into. We went, and as we were about to leave, a mutual friend said, "You cannot leave and not pray for me." We began praying for her when, not long into the prayer, there was a demonic manifestation-a spirit resisted and declared it was not leaving. It threw her on the floor, and after some commands and quoting of scriptures, we expelled that evil spirit. She began crying and seemed embarrassed, or so we thought. The Holy Spirit told me it was not her speaking but a spirit of shame and embarrassment. I began calling out the spirit by name, and it said, "How did you know I was here?"

This one declared it entered through her being embarrassed by her brothers, who ill-treated her whenever she asked for financial assistance. Utilizing our authority, the demon yielded to the power in the name of Jesus. However, another demon manifested itself like a cat. It declared its assignment was from her father, who assigned it in her childhood for her protection. The Holy Spirit then reminded me that cats detest water. No, I did not pour water on her! Nor did I give her water to drink. That would have been useless and occultic. Instead, we began praying that the anointing would flood her life as rivers of water. The power of the Holy Spirit ultimately defeated the evil spirit. To God be the glory, she got delivered that very night.

We have heard and seen many strange things in our ministry with demonized persons. One of the most bizarre occurrences happened in St Thomas, Jamaica, considered by the natives as the island's obeah capital. Some practices among particular residents were diabolical. Some pregnant mothers would go to the 'balm yard' or revival church on a night called 'Healing.' The 'healers' would then give the pregnant women a 'bath' in their concoction to ensure the health and protection of both mother and child. Soon after her child's birth, the mother would insert her finger into her sexual organ and use its fluid to mark an 'X' on the child's forehead for further protection. If the fluid is as potent as these healers professed, the child, coming from the source, should have already been protected. Strange, right?

Doors are open when one embraces (willingly or ignorantly) the works of darkness as good or just mere fun. Emotions and personalities are entangled in harmful activities as doors become opened. The remark that some people make after an evil act is a clear sign of an open door. Comments like, "That is unlike me; I don't know what had come over me," "The Devil made me do it," and "I had no control over myself" are just a few examples. These are not just excuses; in many cases, they are true. Somewhere in their past, a door permitted the demons access, allowing them to do whatever and whenever they wanted through the available vessel.

**Prayer Time**

Lord Jesus, I come to you now acknowledging that there have been opened doors into my life through wilful or ignorant acts. I confess and repent of every activity I would have been involved in to establish these openings. Father God, please forgive me and those who have created these openings. Take away from me every desire for every kind of unrighteousness.

I ask for the Holy Spirit's guidance into wholesome acts glorifying Jesus Christ and His Kingdom. Amen!

# CHAPTER 3
# I DO NOT WANT THIS! WHAT CAN/WILL ENTER?

Ever since conception, humans have faced negative and positive influences. The devil is relentlessly attacking our lives from the womb to the tomb. Our mother's womb is the most significant portion of our innocence, and that state of unconsciousness may be the only time we have no control over what enters our lives. Apart from those times, we are responsible for making the right choices. What individuals choose to partake in may determine what enters. The Bible says, *"As a man thinketh in his heart, so is he" (Proverbs. 23:7).*

James 1:14 says: *"But every man is tempted when he is drawn away of his lust and enticed."* The Devil is aware of our desires (lusts); thus, he knows what to entice us with. In this context, Lust is not speaking of just evil desires but also the fulfillment of these desires. The concept suggests that what you focus on will considerably affect who you are what you do and may become.

The body aligns itself and functions based on the more dominant sense in operation. The smell of your favourite food could cause you to drool, and hearing your favourite music may cause a reaction. Anything treasured in your life will take priority. St. Matthew 6:21 and St. Luke 12:34 say, "For where your treasure is, there will your heart be also." This reality is why you must occupy your heart with the things of God - you can only go where you intend to if you are on the right track. A wise investor will only buy into an asset if they first scope the market. No one studies economics if they want to be a medical doctor. Likewise, you must make the right decisions to guard your body against demonic oppression and possession.

In Genesis 3, we see the fall of man and the resultant curses, which are a direct consequence of impenitence. We see Adam and Eve playing the blame game, with Eve's utterance of the familiar phrase, "The Devil made me do it." While Adam says, "The woman you gave to be with me." Neither of the two admitted to the wrong they had done, but rather deflected it onto someone else.

A curse is God's way of dealing with sin and an effort to bring man into the consciousness of his sin and his need to repent. God is not the one who carries out these curses, but an evil spirit/demon. The Bible writes, *"An evil spirit from God harassed King Saul" (1 Samuel 16:14).* However, note that the Spirit of the Lord departed from Saul, and it was then that an evil spirit from the Lord troubled him. A more appropriate rendering of the scripture implies God allowed an evil spirit to harass Saul. Saul's unremorseful heart was the gateway to his rejection, curse, and possession.

Another scripture that I believe alludes to this is St. Matthew 18:22-35: *"Jesus saith unto him, I say not unto thee, until seven times: but, until seventy times seven. Therefore, is the kingdom of heaven likened unto a certain king, which would take account of his servants. And when he had begun to reckon, one was brought unto him, which owed him ten thousand talents. But forasmuch as he had not to pay, his lord commanded him to be sold, his wife, children, and all he had, and payment to be made. The servant, therefore, fell and worshipped him, saying, Lord, have patience with me, and I will pay thee all. Then the lord of that servant was moved with compassion, loosed him, and forgave him the debt. But the same servant went out and found one of his fellow servants, which owed him a hundred pence: and he laid hands on him, and took him by the throat, saying, Pay me that thou owest. And his fellow servant fell at his feet and besought him, saying, have patience with me, and I will pay thee all. And he would not: but went and cast him into prison, till he should pay the debt. So, when his fellow servants saw what was done, they were very sorry and said to their lord all that was done. Then his lord, after that he had called him, said unto him, O thou wicked servant, I forgave thee all that debt because thou desiredst me: Shouldest, not thou also have had compassion on thy fellow servant, even as I pitied thee? And his lord was worth, and delivered him to the tormentors, till he should pay all that was due unto him. So likewise, shall my heavenly Father do also unto you, if ye from your hearts forgive not everyone his brother their trespasses."*

In this passage, Jesus tells His disciples a story with forgiveness as its moral. The account insinuates that unforgiveness will lead to torment. However, God Himself does not inflict torture, yet He allows it to occur from evil spirits. In James, it says, *"Let no man say when he is tempted, I am tempted of God: for God cannot be tempted with evil, neither tempteth he any man: But every man is tempted, when he is drawn away of his own lust, and enticed."* It is unlike God to do evil, although He allows it.

The account of Job sheds a more excellent light on the subject. The Sons of God came together, and Satan was present among them. The Lord and Satan had a dialogue that led to Job's affliction. God and Satan acknowledged Job's righteousness and regarded him as God's servant, testifying to Job's faithfulness. The Lord presented Job to Satan, but Satan intended to afflict Job. The narrative shows that devotion to the Lord will not nullify Satan's temporal attack but will keep you from the torment of indwelling spirits and hell.

Demons can be transferred from one individual to another through what is known as the transference of spirits. This transfer could happen in numerous ways. A few methods are touching, receiving gifts, covenants, and sexual intercourse. I had mentioned before that the state of a mother during pregnancy could affect the child. An unwanted pregnancy can open the door for a spirit of rejection to enter. The child then grows up struggling with low self-esteem, feelings of inadequacy, rejection, murder, and even suicidal thoughts.

Always bear in mind that whatever power we see being displayed by God, the Devil has a counterfeit to it. The Apostle Paul intimated that a gift could be transferred by laying on of hands when he said that Timothy should stir the gift of God within him, which was imparted to him by the laying of his hands. I urge you to be careful who you allow to lay hands on you, especially on your head. Whatever is in that person, good or evil, could be passed on to you while you are in a receptive mood.

## Recollection #9

A friend called me one day to share her experience. She had received a call from a young lady she had an acquaintance with. The young lady in question had gone to an ordination service in support of her mentor, who was being ordained.

The Chief Consecrator told the young lady that "The Lord" told him some personal things about her, and he needed to minister to her privately, and he proceeded to lay his hands on her and prayed for her. The next morning, she was bent over and in pain. One of the places he laid his hand was also bruised. Upon identifying what had happened - a transference of spirit had occurred - my friend had to administer deliverance to her.

## Recollection #10

My sister, a deliverance minister herself, told me the story of a co-worker who had become mysteriously ill, and doctors could not find the root cause of her complaint. One evening, Christian co-workers visited her and prayed for her healing. While in prayer, one of the visitors saw a carving on the wall and inquired where she had received it. The person prayed for said it was given to her by a friend who had brought it back from a trip to Haiti. The carving was removed from the wall and thrown outside the house, where it fell and hit a rock, broke, and blood came out of it. Her deliverance came, and she was restored to good health by God's power.

Once there is unrepentant sin, there is a potential opening, and evil spirits will be allowed access into our lives. Where we have confessed and repented of our sins, a curse has no power over us. (Proverbs 26:2) An undeserved curse will be powerless to harm you. It may flutter over you like a bird, but it will find no place to land (CEV). Demons travel in groups. For clarity, I suggest you read Frank and Ida-Mae Hammond's book, 'Pigs in the Parlour.' The story of the demoniac at Gadara confirms this. The report stated that the man had a legion of demons (A large group). (St. Mark 5:9) writes: "And he asked him, what is thy name? And he answered, saying,

"My name is Legion, for we are many." A legion is a Roman army term of 6000-foot soldiers (infantry) plus cavalry. Lust must not be taken casually; it can open the door to pornography, masturbation, voyeurism, fornication, etc. Hence, you must not give place to the Devil (Ephesians 4:27).

**Prayer Time**

Father of light, I grant you full access to every dark area of my life. Let Your light shine deep within me, eradicating all levels of darkness. Break every curse from my life and bloodline.

I must be the reflection of Your light in this darkened world. Bind and cast out every force of darkness and grant Me Your freedom to walk in Your light and have daily fellowship with You.

Amen!

# CHAPTER 4
# OOPS! THERE IS A DOOR HERE!
# ARE THERE DOORS AT CHURCH?

Many have considered the Garden of Eden a perfect place, yet the devil entered. Genesis 3:1 state: *"Now the serpent was more subtle than any beast of the field which the LORD God had made. And he said unto the woman, Yea, hath God said, Ye, shall not eat of every tree of the garden?"* Whether the devil possessed the body of a serpent, or he shape-shifted is not central - the text is silent for a reason. What is significant and specific is that the devil was there.

We also read in the Book of Job chapters one and two that Satan presented himself at an angelic conference in heaven. "Now there was a day when the sons of God came to present themselves before the LORD, and Satan also came among them" (Job 1:6). "Again, there was a day when the sons of God came to present themselves before the LORD, and Satan also came among them to present himself before the LORD." (Job 2:1) Again, we see Satan/the Devil in a place that many would consider out-of-bounds for him.

The church (The Body of Christ) is the authorized agency through which God operates to bring true deliverance. Hence, it is the last group on earth; many would think they could become demonized, but guess what? It happens. How can this be? First, let me establish that not all church persons are 'saved,' and not all 'saved' are 'delivered.' I do not limit this to congregants, but laity and clergy alike. God will only control what we surrender to Him.

One school of thought teaches that demons cannot affect Christians. That is not true! A Christian cannot be possessed, as possession speaks of ownership, but they can be oppressed, depressed, and suppressed, depending on the level of control or the lack thereof they give the devil or God, respectively. The analogy of light in a dark room shall shed some light here. Once light hits the darkness, it has to disappear.

Darkness only appears where light has no access. If you close the window of your heart, the light will not shine within. If you have yet to surrender every area of your life to Christ, there is always the possibility that an evil spirit will dwell in your dark places. I have undertaken hundreds of deliverance sessions on persons, from pastors to new converts. Therefore, it behooves every Christian, especially those in active ministry, to be mindful that the devil watches out for an unguarded hour to infiltrate lives. Let us never bring down our defense.

Many germs and bacteria reside in a hospital, given the myriad of diseases and illnesses that pass through its doors. However, constant disinfecting and sterilizing make it a safe environment. That is like the church. No one in the church is perfect, but we are all working towards absolute perfection in Christ, which can happen through consistent disinfecting and sterilizing with the Word of God and through the blood of Jesus. John 17:17 intimates that the saints are sanctified through God's truth, and His Word is truth.

There are even cases that come to the hospital that require quarantining of the infected person so as not to cause a spread of that virus. From time to time, the church should consider quarantining (pulling us from active ministry for counselling and deliverance) those who could contaminate the congregation through ministries. *"That the Father might sanctify them and cleanse them, by the washing of water by the word" (Ephesians 5:26 paraphrased).*

As alluded to earlier, demons can be transferred from one to another during ministry, especially in the case of music and the laying on of hands. Music is a potent force in and of itself. Music, even without lyrics, can make us happy or sad.

*Recollection #11*

One musician testified of his experience with this. As a Christian, he had been visiting nightclubs and inviting the go-go dancers home to have intercourse with them. He testified that the following morning, he would be in church playing. He had been harbouring hurts caused upon his family by people within the church where his dad had been the Pastor.

He said one morning, while playing, he was complaining to God about everything they (as a family) had been through and how members of the congregation had hurt them. Then he heard the voice of the Lord speaking to him, saying, "You have caused more hurt to the assembly than they had done to your family because every time that you went out and committed adultery and went back to church to play the instrument, you released that spirit into the atmosphere".

All those who minister through the performing arts must spend time in the Lord's presence to get a revelation about new songs, sounds, dance moves, etc. Only the Holy Spirit truly knows what God desires. But one thing is for sure: He wants nothing tainted by sin. A B-flat is a B-flat anywhere, anytime; it won't matter who plays it. What makes the difference is the spirit behind who plays it.

The laying-on-of-hands ministry is another easy and unsuspecting way persons can become demonized in church. Some deliverance ministers require deliverance themselves from evil spirits residing in them resulting from private and unconfessed sin. Therefore, this ministry is dangerous and contaminating to the unsuspecting congregant seeking 'deliverance'- the person being ministered to is open to whatever spirits the minister may impart.

I have had the laying of hands on me without my consent on several occasions. My reflex modus operandi is to pray and ask the Father to shield me from evil spirits or negativity that can be transferred to me through this ministry. At that moment, I ask God to forgive me of whatever sins I might not have repented of, so the demons can find no doorway.

A ministerial colleague told me about an incident at the church he was pastoring. He invited a guest speaker, who was laying hands and praying for individuals during his ministry. One of the members ministered to, went to my colleague afterward, and shared what the experience was like for her. She told him that after the guest speaker laid his hands on her and prayed, she felt sexually aroused. Subsequent investigations, carried out by my colleague, revealed that the minister was known for sexual misconduct.

No transference occurred, but the spirit attempted to get her to become lustful toward the guest speaker - who knows what could have followed. She was wise to reject the feeling and seek counsel from her spiritual leader. A hedge is built around you - do not break it!

**Prayer Time**

Almighty God, please help me never break the hedge you have placed around me by going after Satan's entice to satisfy my lusts. Help me not to be ignorant of his evil devices. I commit to consecrate my will and desires in Your hands, oh Heavenly Father. Teach me what to desire and grant me only those. Take away from me every appetite for sin, unrighteousness, or anything that does not bring glory to Your name and could open doors to my life for demons. Dear Father, let Your angels always encamp around me in Jesus' name.

Amen!

# CHAPTER 5
# THE DEVIL IN YOUR SPACE HOW COULD HE BE?

Many Christians believe that because they are filled with the Holy Ghost and speak in tongues, they cannot be affected by demons. Satan is the master of deception, seeking to chart the believers off course. Therefore, it is so important to listen to the voice of the Holy Spirit and obey Him. Demons act on anything available to them - nothing is off limits, not even a casual disagreement with your spouse. Demons are in our space, eagerly waiting for an opening to pounce. I am not talking about you and your spouse arguing or, as my wife and I call it, an "intense moment of fellowship" or the children acting out (though he might very well be acting through them). The Devil can be (and most likely is) in your space. Now, just before you get ready to rebuke me, hear what the scripture says about the Devil and his ability to be in your area and why.

Deception is Satan's most incredible tool. He is a master at getting people to believe a lie. If you accept his lie, you will follow that lie, and Satan will have half his job accomplished. Satan introduced humanity to his trickery. This place was conducive to righteous living, an atmosphere set for God's visitation. The Garden of Eden would have been considered to be the only perfect place on earth, yet Satan was there. What says your house, business, or church? You might say, but this is Earth. Yes, it is! But that was Earth before the fall, spanking new without sin or sinners.

As previously discussed, the Devil was in the Garden of Eden. He was in that "perfect" place up to his trickery. However, while we agree that Satan is not omnipresent, we must be mindful that Satan has a host of cohorts. He has an extensive network of demons at his disposal. So, though he cannot be there in actual presence, he can be there in re-presentation. His mandate to kill, steal, and destroy through the basis of deception is being carried out every day via this network. The Devil occasionally will make special appearances depending on the extremity of the case. Matt. 4:1 said that Jesus was led by the Spirit of God into the wilderness to be tempted by the Devil. He has deceived many into believing there are places he cannot enter or places he has no control over.

Jesus, the Son of God, was fasting and praying when the Devil came on assignment to tempt Him. I want to pause here and tell you this: you must remember, not everything you hear during your time of prayer and fasting will be of/from God. That is why you need to have a "working" knowledge of the scriptures with proper understanding. Also, I would like to bring to the fore that the text said that "the devil" departed from Jesus for a season (Luke 4:13). We are constantly being watched by Satan for an opportune moment to attack.

The Devil can enter and control places, whether by invitation or assignment. For example, Job 1:6-12 (KJV) states: *"Now there was a day when the sons of God came to present themselves before the LORD, and Satan also came among them. And the*

*LORD said unto Satan, whence comest thou? Then Satan answered the LORD and said, from going to and fro in the earth and walking up and down. And the LORD said unto Satan, hast thou considered my servant Job, that there is none like him in the earth, a perfect and an upright man, one that feareth God, and escheweth evil? Then Satan answered the LORD and said, doth Job fear God for nought? Hast, not thou made a hedge about him, his house, and all he hath on every side? Thou hast blessed the work of his hands, and his substance is increased in the land. But put forth thine hand now, and touch all that he hath, and he will curse thee to thy face. And the LORD said unto Satan, behold, all that he hath is in thy power; only upon himself put not forth thine hand. So, Satan went forth from the presence of the LORD."*

Job seems to be the text for this book, but there is much truth to glean from his experience; we cannot ignore them. The text gives some insight into Satan and God's relationship:

(i) He congregates with angels. (verse 6)

(ii) He was in the presence of God. (verses 6 and 12)

(iii) He converses with God. (verses 6-12)

(iv) He traverses the earth. (verse 7)

(v) He has desires to destroy the saints (Verse 9-12).

(vi) He has limitations (Verse 12)

(vii) He gets his assignment from God (Verse 12).

So, we can take from this text that some of Satan's accesses result from a direct assignment from God. I firmly believe that as the people of God, the devil cannot touch us without God's permission or unless we choose to leave under God's covering. The blood of Jesus, the armor, and a host of angels protect us. However, what the devil does, as James alludes to in his Epistle, is that he tempts us with the things we desire. Not necessarily that the desire in and of itself is wrong, but rather, how we seek to fulfill it. So, while God will allow some of our troubles, we must remember that the Devil is rebellious and will want to do his own thing after being given access.

Another powerful example of the Devil being in our space is in Luke 4 and Matthew 4, the temptation of Jesus. In both renditions of the account, the statement is made that the Spirit led Jesus into the wilderness to be tempted. Matthew's account gives the impression that after the fast, Satan came and tempted Jesus. Luke gives a different spin. He said, "Being forty days tempted." Let me say that whether during or after our fast, the devil watches for an opportunity to attack us.

Jesus, the Son of God, was fasting and praying when the Devil came to tempt Him. It's important to remember that not everything you hear during your time of prayer and fasting will be from God. That's why it's crucial to have a good understanding of the scriptures. Additionally, it's worth noting that the text mentions that "the devil" departed from Jesus for a season (Luke 4:13). This indicates that we are constantly being watched by Satan, who looks for opportune moments to attack. Having read Job and Jesus' experiences, I recognize Satan will try us because God will assign him to do so. I am more confident going through my situations because they originated *in God, and He has no plans to kill me. Jeremiah 11:29 declares: "For I know the thoughts that I think toward you, saith the LORD, thoughts of peace, and not of evil, to give you an expected end."* Paul writes in Rom 8:28: *"And we know all things work together for good to them that love God, to them who are the called according to his purpose."* James 1:2-4 states: *"My brethren, count it all joy when ye fall into divers temptations; Knowing this, that the trying of your faith worketh patience. But let patience have her perfect work, that ye may be perfect and entire, wanting nothing."* 1Peter 4:12–13, *"Beloved, think it not strange concerning the fiery trial which is to try you, as though some strange thing happened unto you: But rejoice, inasmuch as ye are partakers of Christ's sufferings; that, when his glory shall be revealed, ye may be glad also with exceeding joy."*

There are other examples of the Devil being in our spaces. Jude tells the story of Satan and Michael, the Archangel, disputing over the body of Moses. Jude 1:9: *"Now when Michael, one of the chief angels, was fighting against the Evil One for the body of Moses, fearing to make use of violent words against him, he only said, May the Lord be your judge".* (BBE). Jesus rebuked his disciple Peter because Satan had inspired him to speak against the plan of God concerning Jesus' crucifixion. Mark 8:33: *"But when he had turned about and looked on his disciples, he rebuked Peter, saying, get thee behind me, Satan: for thou savourest not the things that be of God, but the things that be of men."*

Now, another way the Devil gets into our space is by invitation. What do I mean by invitation? Through the doorway of unconfessed/unrepented sins, an invitation is extended (and he is not passing it up). We can come into an experience in the manifested presence of the Lord with our sins and leave with them. It is our choice. The best thing to do when confronted with sin is to admit, confess, and repent. That way, the Devil will have no space in our lives. When King Saul was confronted by the Prophet Samuel concerning the Amalekites, he tried to justify his sin. That opened the door for an evil spirit to torment him, and he ultimately lost the kingdom (read 1 Sam. 15).

Judas was in the presence of Jesus at the last supper table when Satan entered his heart. *"When Jesus had thus said, he was troubled in spirit, and testified, and said, Verily, verily, I say unto you, that one of you shall betray me. Then the disciples looked one on another, doubting of whom he spoke. Now, there was leaning on Jesus' bosom one of his disciples, whom Jesus loved. Simon Peter, therefore, beckoned him to ask who it should be of whom he spake. He then, lying on Jesus' breast, saith unto him, Lord, who is it? Jesus answered, he it is, to whom I shall give a sop when I have dipped it. And when he had dipped the sop, he gave it to Judas Iscariot, the son of Simon. And after the sop, Satan entered him. Then said Jesus unto him, that thou doest, do quickly." (John 13:21-27)*

What had happened manifested what was already in Judas' heart. Sin begins in the heart or mind, and then there is a manifestation in the flesh if not dealt with in its embryonic stage. Mathew 15:19 declares *"For out of the heart come evil thoughts, murder, adultery, sexual immorality, theft, false witness, slander."* Proverbs 23:7, *"For as he thinketh in his heart, so is he: Eat and drink, saith he to thee; but his heart is not with thee."*

Matthew 18:21-35 tells a story about a man turned over to the tormentors because of unforgiveness. Sin brings torment, i.e., sleepless nights, sickness and diseases, loss of property, anger, rage, and loss of peace. Therefore, the best thing to do with sin is to get rid of it as soon as you recognize it.

**Prayer Time**

Father, in the mighty name of Jesus Christ, may I never become complacent on my watch. Grant me the gift of discerning spirits that I may be aware of the devil in my space.

I solicit the grace to overcome his temptations and stand against his wiles no matter in what guise he appears. Help me, dear God, to never be a facilitator of his presence anywhere I am.

I declare all doors shut to him, and I stand guard with the help of our angels assigned to encamp around me as I continue to fear you.

Amen!

# CHAPTER 6
# BREAKING THE CHAINS
# CAN I TRULY BE FREE?

Everyone can, but not everyone will be free from Satan's oppressive sway. Ignorance plays a pivotal role in whether one is delivered or not. Those who genuinely seek to be free must remain progressive with their choice.

People generally don't become demonized by just sinning; the repeated sinning and being unrepentant swings the door open. The devil brings enticement that coincides with your lusts/desires and tempts you to satisfy that desire illegitimately. The progression is lust, temptation, sin, becoming demonized, and ultimately, death.

The first step in this process of deliverance is to be informed. Knowledge is the first rung on the ladder out of the pit. Lack of knowledge of the word of God is a remarkably high price. "My people are destroyed because they do not know. You priests have refused to learn, so I will refuse to let you be priests for me. You have forgotten the law of your God so that I will forget your children" (Hosea 4:6 ERV).

The Bible is our manual on how, as human beings, we ought to live and relate to each other and God. Without this knowledge, we become susceptible to Satan's deception. It is the truth that will set us free. *"Sanctify them through thy truth, thy word is truth" (John 17:17)*. *"Wherewithal shall a young man cleanse his way? By taking heed thereto according to thy word" (Psalm 119;9)*. *"The entrance of thy words giveth light; it giveth understanding unto the simple" (Psalm 119:130)*.

The second rung is honesty, admitting you are in sin and need the Saviour and Deliverer. *"If we confess our sins, He is faithful and just to forgive us our sins, and to cleanse us from all unrighteousness" (1 John 1:9)*. *"Confess your faults one to another, and pray one for another, that ye may be healed. The effectual fervent prayer of a righteous man availeth much" (1 John 1:9)*. One healed of any disease or sickness, must have been honest with the doctor concerning whatever symptoms they are experiencing. Wrong medication is not always because of a doctor's misdiagnosis but a lack of honesty from the patient. Repentance is the third rung. While the word repent means an about-face or godly sorrow for sin, there is a twist that I would like to put on it. The prefix "Re" means to do over or to do again. The suffix "Pent" means 5, the number of grace or provision. God's provision of grace brings us back to our original state. Pent also speaks of height as a penthouse. We have sinned and fallen short of the glory of God, but through repentance, we have been restored to where we are seated in heavenly places in Christ, far above principality.

Forgiveness is a significant key in this process. As mentioned in a previous chapter, a man in the eighteenth chapter of the book of Matthew refused to forgive someone who owed him some money just after someone else had forgiven him for the same reason. The Bible said he was turned over to the tormentor because of this unforgiving spirit. Sin undealt with can lead to emotional and mental distress – torment. I would ask you to do some introspection now and see if you are harbouring this spirit because of anyone, including yourself. You see, many of us can forgive others easily, but as for ourselves, that is a challenge.

The devil is a mentalist, tending to mess with people's minds, convincing them that they caused their dilemma. He plagues the mind with statements such as: "I should have known better," "If only I had just," and "If only I had not." As a result of the devil's scheming ploy, quite a few people's minds have become warped into believing they are the ones to be blamed. Therefore, they will require transformative counselling in the Word of God to renew their mindset. Note: Nothing is impossible with God. Hallelujah!

Unforgiveness is like a handcuff. It keeps individuals emotionally trapped and affected by the offender and the offense until they genuinely decide to let go and forgive. Unfortunately, many of the people who caused the hurt did not know they had done so. Too many people struggle with the spirit of offense, even after the one who offended (knowingly or unknowingly) has moved on. You know that you have sincerely forgiven your offender/s when you can see him/her/them and not recall the hurt. Only then can you say I am FREE! Glory to God! Hallelujah! Thank you, Jesus.

While having knowledge, confessing, forgiving, and repenting are all important. There must be a process of expulsion or casting out of these spirits; this starts with the prayer of renunciation. To renounce is to reject or abandon. In this prayer, one is severing ties with the Devil, sin, and the works of darkness. Thus, the individual lets Satan know their choice to have no more lot or part with him and his cohorts but has Jesus Christ in total control of their entire life.

Acknowledging dirt and talking about it does not remove it. We have to be intentional about our freedom from the weight, guilt, and power of sin. 1 John 1:9 says: *"If we confess our sin, He is faithful and just to forgive us our sins and to cleanse us from all unrighteousness."* Our part is to confess, and his part is to forgive and cleanse. In other words, have the dirt removed.

Here is an example of what a renunciation prayer is like:

## *Prayer of Refusal against Satan*

Lord Jesus, I pray for myself and my family (name them); I commit our lives to you totally: bodies, souls, and spirits. I ask that You bend, break, and mold us to make us into who You want us to be.

Satan, I come against you and all your hosts; I reject and refuse all the snares, pits, and traps you have set up to draw us away from the Lord, Jesus Christ, and deliverance. Satan, I rebuke, reject, renounce, resist, and sever any contact and soul ties to you and your hosts in the name of the Lord Jesus Christ.

I disannul any contract signed, consciously or unconsciously, and declare them null and void. Then, as an act of my conscious will, I take back every ground I yielded to you, Satan, and surrender them to the Lordship of Jesus Christ.

I decree that every demonic spirit indwelling me would be expelled from my life. I command the spirits of (name them) to leave me now in the name of Jesus Christ.

Father, I ask for Your best in our lives today, that Your will and purpose be done in and through us. Keep us in your perfect will as yielded vessels for your work. Today, we bring you honour, praise, glory, blessing, and joy. Amen!

Let me caution that self-deliverance is possible and sometimes suggested. However, it is not the safest practice. Sometimes, in the process, there will be manifestations that the person being delivered cannot handle on their own. E.g., the shutting down of the physical being or a convulsion that could end in injury. Matt 9:14-29 records the story of a boy with an epileptic spirit who had often been thrown into the fire and water by this spirit wanting to destroy him.

I strongly recommend getting help from someone experienced in the Ministry of Deliverance to guide one through this process. God is highly concerned about one's spiritual well-being, complete freedom, and victory over the powers of darkness. That is why Christ paid the ultimate price. As a result, Satan was officially defeated when Christ cried out on the cross, "It is finished!" After which, He took the keys of "authority" over death and hell. Therefore, Satan will remain defeated even after the rapture of the church. So do not let Jesus' death for you be in vain - His delivering grace is yours to access by faith in Him alone.

Deliverance does not require drinking "consecrated" water or olive oil. Jesus Christ used his authority and spoke the Word. Every believer has power over demons and the works of Satan. Doing some of these things is just an act of appeasing the demons. You risk making covenants with demons when you get involved in extra-biblical practices.

**Prayer Time**

Almighty God and my Father, I thank You for Your love and mercy extended to me. Today, Lord, I come to You seeking Your help in this process of being and staying free from the works of darkness. Issues have trapped me in a place that is less than You have designed me to live. Holy Spirit, please guide me into the truth of God's deliverance. I choose to be accessible by following the steps outlined in this chapter. First, I acknowledge my sins, confess and repent of them all. Then, Second, I consciously decide to forgive everyone who has ever offended me. I sever myself from every demonic activity and renounce any relations with them. I declare that I have no more lot nor part with the unfruitful works of darkness. I walk away from unrighteousness and embrace the righteousness provided to me by Your Son's death, burial, and resurrection.

Hallelujah and amen!

# CHAPTER 7
# GIVE ME THOSE KEYS! KEYS GRANT OR DENY ACCESS

*"Satan is a sly old fox; if I could catch him, I would put him in a box. Lock that box and throw away the key for all those tricks he played on me."*

Yes, I know you smiled as that song reminded you about your Sunday/Sabbath school days.

Keys are synonymous with authority – the power of granting or denying access. There are many acceptable ways of entering a building today. Keys, swipe cards, remotes, body sensors, and other forms of biometrics can grant access. However, access must come from a place or position of authority. Any other way of entry would be deemed illegal. John 10:1; *"Verily, verily, I say unto you, He that entereth not by the door into the sheepfold, but climbeth up some other way, the same is a thief and a robber."*

Likewise, access points, vortexes, or portals to the supernatural realm require approval (from a legal regulator) to gain entry. I have discussed this in my other book, 'Accessing the Supernatural Realm.'

When God created man, He made Him in the God class to operate like Him. He then placed him in the garden east of Eden. He declared to him that he should have dominion. Dominion speaks to possessing authority. So, you could say Adam had the keys to the Garden of Eden and, by extension, the Earth. So, Elohim made man the guardian of the planet in partnership with Him, the supreme ruler.

God's archenemy, Satan, with His cunning nature, deceived man into relinquishing his authority to him by seducing him to wanting to be more than he already was. The man was overseeing the earth, but Satan deceived him that he could be more. Adam was tricked into believing he could be like God, the creator–Elohim. The discourse concluded with Adam losing his authority/keys to rule the garden and, ultimately, Earth. He was, therefore, displaced from the garden, and God appointed a new keeper and assigned angels to watch over it with what seemed like 'laser beams.' *"So, he drove out the man, and he placed at the east of the garden of Eden Cherubims, and a flaming sword which turned every way, to keep the way of the tree of life." (Genesis 3:24)*

That was not the end of the story, as God had a redemption plan from before the earth's foundation that Satan was not privy to. I have listed a few scriptures below for reflection:

*"And all that dwell upon the earth shall worship him, whose names are not written in the book of life of the Lamb slain from the foundation of the world." (Revelation 13:8)*

*"For God so loved the world that He gave His only begotten Son, that whosoever believeth on Him should not perish but have everlasting life" (John 3:16).*

*"Howbeit we speak wisdom among them that are perfect: yet not the wisdom of this world, nor the princes of this world, that come to naught: But we speak the wisdom of God in a mystery, even the hidden wisdom, which God ordained before the world unto our glory: Which none of the princes of this world knew: for had they known it, they would not*

*have crucified the Lord of glory" (1 Corinthians 2:6-8).*

Elohim is the consummate project manager – He already had a contingent plan. Man's fall did not surprise Him; he knew it would happen and planned for it. One word used to describe this process is regeneration. Paligenesia in Greek is a compound word derived from the roots Palin and Genesis. Palin means to anew, and Genesis means nativity or nature. *Paligenesia*, or its English equivalent, *regeneration*, represents a new nature. *"Therefore, if any man is in Christ, he is a new creature: old things are passed away; behold, all things have become new" (2 Corinthians 5:17).*

It gets interesting when you break down the word regenerate into syllables. "Re" means to do over or to do again. "Gen" speaks of birth or kind, nature, or nativity. Gene is the basic physical and functional unit of heredity. Genes comprise DNA. And finally, "'rate" relates to the value placed on something. So, we can see our lives have obtained a new value through bearing the genes or DNA of God. *"For as many as are led by the Spirit of God, these are sons of God. For you did not receive the spirit of bondage again to fear but received the Spirit of adoption by whom we cry out, Abba, Father." (Romans 8:14–15)*

*"But as many, as received Him, to them, He gave the right to become children of God, to those who believe in His name" (John 1:12). "Behold what manner of love the Father has bestowed on us, that we should be called children of God" (1 John 3:1).*

Jesus said to Peter (Mat 16:18-19): *"And I also say unto thee, that thou art Peter, and upon this rock, I will build my church; and the gates of hell shall not prevail against it. And I will give unto thee the keys of the kingdom of heaven: and whatsoever thou shalt bind on earth shall be bound in heaven: and whatsoever thou shalt loose on earth shall be loosed in heaven."* It is essential at this juncture to point out that Jesus said, *"I will,"* and not I have. Jesus spoke in the future tense. He was intimating that His death and resurrection would be inevitable. When He rose from the dead and appeared to the disciples, He said, *"Peace be unto you: as my Father hath sent me, even so, send I you. And when he had said this, he breathed on them, and saith unto them, Receive ye the Holy Ghost." (John 20:21-22)*

Here are a few things to remember: Firstly, when the Spirit came, He came with POWER. *"But ye shall receive power, after that the Holy Ghost comes upon you: and ye shall be witnesses unto me both in Jerusalem, and in all Judaea, and in Samaria, and unto the uttermost part of the earth." (Acts 1:8)* The word 'power' in the text is the Greek word dunamis which signifies 'force,' 'miraculous power' or 'ability.' Secondly, when the Spirit came, He came to indwell us. *"Even the Spirit of truth; whom the world cannot receive, because it seeth him not, neither knoweth him: but ye know him; for He dwelleth with you and shall be in you." (John 14:17)* While Jesus was on earth they knew him as Emmanuel when interpreted means "God with us" but when the Holy Ghost came and began to indwell man, He was now God in us. Thirdly, because He is now God in us, and we are born again of the Spirit, we have the DNA of God in us, being restored or regenerated to our original state before the fall.

Putting it all together, we see that the information in the gospel of Jesus Christ transforms us. In acceptance of this information, we are born again, and the spiritual gene of God is placed in us, causing us to have new life. 2 Corinthians 5:17 states, *"Therefore, if any man be in Christ, he is a new creature: old things are passed away; behold, all things are become new."* We have the life of God in us that gives us the power to become the sons of God.

St. Luke 10:19 writes: *"Behold, I give unto you the power to tread on serpents and scorpions, and over all the power of the enemy: and nothing shall by any means hurt you."* The word power is used twice in the text, but does not mean the same thing. The first use is the Greek word exousia, which means 'delegated influence' or 'authority.' The second, as we said before, means 'ability.' Hence, Jesus was speaking to the disciples that He gave them authority over all the abilities of Satan. That sounds like the restoration of the keys/authority to man.

Jesus, through His death, burial, and resurrection, obtained victory over sin, death, hell, and the grave. In this, He also returned the rightful rulership of the earth into man's hands. He would not have done this without us first being regenerated. You and I, as born-again believers, are new creatures in

Christ, and those endowed with the POWER of the Holy Spirit, are possessors of the keys/authority of the earth. Let us live like it.

**Prayer Time**

Great King of the Heavens and the Earth, I bow in Your incredible presence, acknowledging Your supreme rulership. Your authority extends to the end of the universe. I thank You for the knowledge now given to me concerning my authority in the supernatural realm. I, therefore, stand in it and declare my victory over the works of darkness. Today, by the authority invested in me, I take back every ground I have yielded to Satan. As an act of submission to Your Lordship, I surrender my will and choice to you. I am wholly Yours for Your honour and glory. I close every door opened to satan and grant You full access to my life.

Amen!

# CHAPTER 8
# AGREE WITH YOUR ADVERSARY
# HOW IMPORTANT IS THIS?

Matthew 5:25 states, *"Agree with thine adversary quickly whiles thou art in the way with him; lest at any time the adversary deliver thee to the judge, and the judge deliver thee to the officer, and thou be cast into prison."*

This text is part of a larger discourse called the Sermon on the Mount. It was during His delivery on Christian character that Jesus spoke these words. But what does it mean to agree with our adversary? What does that look like? How is it even done? How is it beneficial to our Christian walk?

## Recollection # 10

A friend shared his experience agreeing with his "adversary" and how it worked out in his favour. He had received a traffic ticket in the mail indicating that he ran a red light, and he had no recollection of doing so and was going to court to contest it. While mentally preparing to defend himself, the Lord told him to admit to the wrong. This situation was part of God's plan to teach him a valuable lesson. So, he did admit to guilt, and in his admission of guilt, the judge dropped the charges.

Agreeing with our adversary simply means admitting to our wrongs/sins. It is in the admission of guilt that we agree with our adversary. It is not about becoming covenant partners to do evil. Confession of sin is the first step in being declared free from the guilt of sin. 1 John 1:9 states: *"If we confess our sins, he is faithful and just to forgive us our sins and to cleanse us from all unrighteousness."* Confession equals admission.

Conviction leads to confession, confession to repentance, repentance to forgiveness, forgiveness to deliverance, and deliverance to freedom.

When we read the bible at a glance, we gloss over many truths that will set us free when applied. Knowledge is not power if not used. While reading St. Luke 18:1, *"then He spoke a parable to them, that men always ought to pray and not lose heart,"*. The word "ought" stood out to me. So, I quickly researched and discovered that it was a legal term, and it says we are legally bound to pray for things to happen in this earthly realm. Note that the story told after that verse was a legal matter.

I became more aware that God's Word has many legal terms. Words such as petition, judge, advocate, confess, judgment, plead, punishment, accuser, etc. The Bible describes Satan as the *"Accuser of the brethren" Rev. 12:10.* His modus operandi is to tempt us, and when we yield to his temptation, he goes before God to accuse us. Letting the just judge know that He cannot release what is legally ours to us because we broke the covenant. We have done something illegal, therefore forfeiting our blessing.

Some propagate that there is such a thing as a generational blessing, but deny the opposite. Understand that God told Abraham, *"I will bless them that bless thee, and curse them that curse thee."* If there can be a generational blessing, then the converse is true.

The devil will attack from both a legal and an illegal perspective. If the attack is illegal, we already have the power to nullify it. When it is legal, we must go to the court of heaven to have the matter dealt with by the Just Judge.

How does it all work? Satan brings an accusation against us before God because we have yielded to his temptation to sin. God, who is just, cannot release what is legally ours to us because there is a matter in the court that must be addressed. We go before the court in admission of guilt, i.e., agreeing with our adversary. Confessing and repenting of that sin and pleading the blood of Jesus, the advocate, as our defense.

The case, through the power of the name and blood of Jesus, is dismissed, and we can now stand justified. Romans 8:33 says, *"Who will bring any charge against those whom God has chosen? It is God who justifies."* Satan's legal rights are given to him through our sins, and our admission and repentance of guilt removes his diabolical power. Now, we have the authority and ability that the court of heaven granted us to destroy every demonic stronghold from ourselves and our family.

But that is not all we can do. We can now request a restraining order against the adversary, denying him access to that area of our lives. "This is a restraining or protective order issued by the court of Heaven to protect a person's destiny, institution, business, national institutions involving clear and present dangers to the pre-ordained purposes of God," Dr. Myles Francis. An example of this may be found in the book of Numbers 22. God is the one responsible for the enforcement. Note that He was the one who made the donkey talk to Balaam. This order will keep the door closed. However, we must keep them closed by not yielding to the devil's next temptations.

I also recommend that we seek a gag order to keep him from bringing up the issue in future conversations. A Gag Order is when the court/judge prohibits the lawyers, parties, or witnesses from publicly mentioning anything about the case. When we ask for a gag order, we restrict Satan and his emissary from spreading information about us or to others. Let us use the court of heaven to maintain our freedom from satanic bondage.

If we search our lives, we find that many situations are cyclical. Finances, health, relationships, psychological highs, and lows permeate our lives. There is a constant battle going on. Today, we are up, and by nightfall, we are down. We pray and fast, and the cycle continues and, at times, gets more intense. Those of us living in the tropics can appreciate the value of rooting up a tree instead of trimming it if we want to eliminate it. Trimming it allows it to grow back stronger. Going to the final court of appeal gets to the root of the matter and destroys its stronghold in our lives.

**Prayer time**

Righteous judge of all, I am grateful to you for your grace in times of trouble. I admit that sometimes I do not do things according to your standards. This way of living often opens the doors to the adversary seeking full advantage to accuse me before your throne. Please forgive me of every sin the accuser now stands before you, presenting as a case against me.

I repent and nullify his legal rights to bring a case in your court. I plead the blood of Jesus as my defense, appropriate it to my life, and claim my freedom. I will not be a slave to sin.

Amen!

# CHAPTER 9
# BREAK DOWN THAT ALTAR

We have read numerous stories in the Bible that speak to the construction and destruction of altars. Two of the more well-known stories are those of Gideon and Elijah. God instructed Gideon to tear down his father's Baal altar and erect an altar unto Him, Jehovah. (Judges 6). Elijah went into a head-on spiritual confrontation with the prophets of Baal, who ate at Jezebel's table in a battle of the altars (1 Kings 18). When we understand an altar and its role in our everyday reality, we will greatly appreciate its significance and how it can affect our lives.

An altar is one of the places that are integral to any religion. The altar is the place where worship of any deity occurs. Also, the proponents of that religion believe that performing certain rituals at the altar will invoke the blessing of said deity. We get married, christened, ordained, and commissioned at an altar. You may then ask the question, why is an altar so important? This altar is a place of transformation.

Let us explore a few definitions of an altar. (1) A place of transaction or exchange, (2) A portal or landing strip, (3) A place where the natural meets the supernatural, (4) A place where sacrifice is offered, (5) A place of worship, (6) A corridor into the supernatural realm, (7) A system of authorization.

I believe the first act of illicit worship in the Bible was when Eve obeyed Satan in Eden. Because she followed Satan and sinned against God, she offered her worship to Satan, which would have been an invisible altar. An exchange took place between Eve and Satan, and she took his sin, sickness, darkness, etc., in exchange for her holiness, health, and light. Romans 6:16 States: *"Know ye not, that to whom ye yield yourselves servants to obey, his servants ye are to whom ye obey; whether of sin unto death, or of obedience unto righteousness?"*

We are all victims or victors through encounters with altars. There are two types of altars: evil and righteous. Wherever worship occurs is an altar, whether stationary or portable, visible, or invisible. The one to whom we obey is the one whose spirit controls us. Whether we consciously or unconsciously worship, we surrender to the lord of the altar at which we bow.

Altars are constructed for varied purposes. When we look at the Old Testament, we see many leaders erecting altars. Abraham alone built four altars in Genesis 12:1-7. Praise and thanksgiving for the pronouncement of blessings. Gen. 12:8-13 Prayer, where he called upon God. Gen. 13: 14-18 Peace ended the strife between his and Lot's herders. Gen. 22: 19-14 Provision, the Lord provided a ram in Isaac's stead.

The construction of an altar is not limited to space, place, size, or realm. An altar can be built in your home, at your workplace, in your car, in the woods, on the mountain tops, or even by a river. In ancient times, worshippers constructed altars of stone, wood, or earth to offer worship. What was most significant was to whom the worshipper presented on that altar.

Abraham built an altar in Genesis 15 during the encounter with God in which God promised him a son and that his seed would inherit the land of Canaan. Isaac built an altar in Genesis 26, where he called on the name of the Lord. This situation occurred when he and Abimelech strived over the wells. It was not until Isaac built an altar and called on God that the strife ceased. Gideon made three altars when the angel of the Lord visited him in Ophrah, Judges 6:20, 24, & 26.

We observed from these few references that an altar is in the picture whenever an encounter with the supernatural occurs. Evil altars are not different in their significance, and they serve as portals into the unseen realm to carry out evil agendas. The story of Balaam and Balak in the Book of Numbers relates how Balak, the King of Moab, called Balaam, the prophet, to curse Israel. Both made a total of 21 altars to curse Israel. A feat that was impossible at the time, as Israel was in the right standing with God. The intent was to annihilate Israel. However, the altar of God is superior; hence, their efforts were of no effect.

## **Knowing how to destroy and disassociate ourselves from evil altars is essential.**

How do we destroy the evil altar? Exo 34:10 - 17 (NLT) *Then the Lord said, "I am making this agreement with all of your people. I will do amazing things that have never before been done for any other nation on earth. The people with you will see that I, the LORD, am very great. They will see the wonderful things that I will do for you. Obey what I command you today, and I will force your enemies to leave your land. I will force out the Amorites, Canaanites, Hittites, Perizzites, Hivites, and Jebusites. Be careful! Don't make any agreement with the people who live in the land where you are going. If you make an agreement with them, it will bring you trouble. So, destroy their altars, break the stones they worship, and cut down their idols. Don't worship any other god. I am YAHWEH KANAH-THE JEALOUS LORD. That is my name. I hate for my people to worship other gods. "Be careful not to make any agreements with the people who live in that land. If you do this, you might join them when they worship their gods. They will invite you to join them, and you will eat their sacrifices. You might choose some of their daughters as wives for your sons. Those daughters serve false gods. They might lead your sons to do the same thing. "Don't make idols.*

YAHWEH KANAH had spoken to Moses concerning what could transpire in the land of their possession and advised him to be careful not to allow the children of Israel to participate in any idolatrous act. There is a series of steps in destroying an evil altar that will produce success. None of these steps should be ignored or treated as slight. All are significant to the demolishing of evil altars from our lives.

1. Do not praise your ancestors for their sins. In doing so, it connects you to the altar. Many people are not directly involved in establishing evil altars but seek to benefit from them. They will speak glowingly of what their ancestors have done and claim it as their source of protection or blessings.
2. Do not boast about the evil that your ancestors did. Consider it a sin and separate yourself

from such practices or their results. The devil always disguises a curse as a blessing. God never gives a curse in the guise of a wholesome gift. His benefits are clean and clear of evil. *"The blessing of the Lord maketh rich and addeth no sorrow to it."*

NOTE: Genuine repentance, a godly sorrow for ancestral and personal sins, breaks the power of an evil altar. Destruction of the altar stops the altar from speaking against you. Disassociate yourself from anything of your ancestors, whether they be valuable or sentimental.

3. Destroy the evil altar in the heart. The heart is where altars are established first. *St. Matthew 12:34; "O generation of vipers, how can ye, being evil, speak good things? for out of the abundance of the heart the mouth speaketh." St. Luke 6:45 "A good man out of the good treasure of his heart bringeth forth that which is good; and an evil man out of the evil treasure of his heart*

*bringeth forth that which is evil: for of the abundance of the heart his mouth speaketh." Proverbs 4:23; "Keep thy heart with all diligence; for out of it are the issues of life."* These scriptures and others pointedly address the issue of heart health. As in the natural, so in the spiritual. The healthier the organ that pumps the blood through-out your system, the healthier the body. Likewise, the healthier your spirit, the healthier your life. Therefore, we must pay attention to what we allow into our spirits.

4. Plead your case in the courts of heaven. We would have covered this point sufficiently in the previous chapter. However, let me remind you that we must deprive satan of every legal ground to access our lives. We can counter-sue and apply for a restraining order against the satanic hosts through the courts of heaven.

5. Raise a righteous altar in your heart. In the Old Testament, altars were physical places with a structure upon which persons

offered sacrifices. In the New Testament, the heart is where the altar is. This prayer altar finds expression in a place, a posture, and practice. There is a place where one feels most comfortable encountering God-where one would have met Him.
6. Sow a sacrificial offering. An offering seals the deal. Altars are of no purpose without an offering. This offering can be of any sort unless God requires something specific of you.

**Prayer Time**

Father God, I thank you for your manifested love for me. I now renounce and sever myself from all demonic altars erected by me or my ancestors. They have no more power over my life as I submit myself to your Lordship. I break down every satanic altar in my heart and sanctify it so you may have the preeminence here. Take residence on the throne/altar of my heart, in Jesus.

Amen!

# CHAPTER 10
# FREE AT LAST
# HOW DO I KEEP MY FREEDOM?

One issue some believers grapple with is the need to be more practical. Everything for them is prayer, Bible reading, and speaking in tongues. They seem to forget that obedience is an act, not some mental gymnastics. Some situations call for practical physical actions and decisions to be made and adhered to. Like Joseph physically ran from Potiphar's wife.

Joshua had to search the camp of Israel to find who had sinned, causing the army's defeat against Ai. They had just conquered a more robust city-Jericho and were now greatly embarrassed by this defeat. As the commander-in-chief, Joshua had to get to the bottom of this. The search ensued, and Achan was found to be the culprit. He and his family subsequently died as that was the prescribed way of dealing with the freedom to come to the Nation. (Joshua 7)

A deep personal relationship with the Godhead is the foundation on which one must stand to keep his freedom. There will be satanic storms that will blow to trap you back in his oppressive snares. See the Father for who He is: (i) The Creator of all things (including Satan). (ii) The giver of ALL good gifts. See Jesus as His Son and our Redeemer, the Way, the Truth, and the Life. Never forget the Holy Spirit is our Comforter, Counsellor, and Guide into ALL truth.

All relationships must have two critical elements to develop: time spent and conversations. The more time you spend conversing, the more revelation and understanding of who you are and to whom you relate will be known. The more we know, understand, and love the Godhead, the less we will sin and disappoint the Godhead and hurt ourselves in the process. The Bible is the principal source of this knowledge and understanding. It is imperative, therefore, that we read, study, and know the Bible, but most importantly, make application thereof. It is the autobiography of the Godhead. When I was in Bible

College, one lecturer (Dr Samuel Vassell) on the first day made this introductory statement (holding up the bible): "You see this book. Read this book and believe this book because it is true." He was my New Testament Survey lecturer who had studied the New Testament in the land of the Bible.

We can always emphasize prayer! There is a catchy expression that holds a wealth of truth I would like to share with you: *"If you do not pray, you cannot stay. If you do not fast, you will not last."* Jesus recommended prayer and fasting to deal with specific situations. In Mark 9:29, Jesus told the disciples that "this kind can come forth by nothing, but by prayer and fasting." Jesus, as our example, fasted and prayed to the Father often during His earthly ministry. He even had some all-nighters thrown in there. *"And it came to pass in those days, that he went out into a mountain to pray, and continued all night in prayer to God." (Luke 6:12).* There are some situations that the Spirit will lead you into, and there are others that the devil draws us into by enticement. We must pray to discern whether we find ourselves in self-invited trouble because of sin or a test orchestrated by God. The Spirit led Jesus into the wilderness.

Luke 4:1-13: *"And Jesus being full of the Holy Ghost returned from Jordan, and was led by the Spirit into the wilderness, being forty days tempted of the devil. And in those days, he ate nothing; when they were ended, he hungered. And the devil said unto him, if thou be the Son of God, command this stone that it be made bread. And Jesus answered him, saying, It is written, That man shall not live by bread alone, but by every word of God. And the devil, taking him up into a high mountain, showed him all the world's kingdoms in a moment. And the devil said unto him, all this power will I give thee, and the glory of them: for that is delivered unto me; and to whomsoever I will, I give it. If thou, therefore, wilt worship me, all shall be thine. And Jesus answered and said unto him, get thee behind me, Satan: for it is written, Thou shalt worship the Lord thy God, and him only shalt thou serve. And he brought him to Jerusalem and set him on a pinnacle of the temple, and said unto him, if thou be the Son of God, cast thyself down from hence: For it is written, He shall give his angels charge over thee, to keep thee: And in their hands, they shall bear thee up, lest at any time thou dash thy foot against a stone. And Jesus answering said unto him, it is said, Thou shalt not tempt the Lord thy God. And when the devil had ended all the temptation, he departed from him for a season."*

The story of Jesus' temptation by the devil is for our learning. What does that mean for us if the devil could have approached the Son of God? If the devil knew the Son of God's needs, what say you and me? If the devil could come to Him at what some would consider a high point in His spiritual sojourn, why not you and me? What wouldn't he do when confronting us if the devil could misrepresent the Word to Jesus?

Remember, this story started with Jesus' baptism in the River Jordon. While He was coming out of the water, the Spirit of God came upon Him. He received words of affirmation. Then, He was led by the same Spirit into the wilderness. Satan, who tempted Jesus, met Him, but Jesus availed Himself to the Spirit so the Spirit could use His sword to defend Him. The Word of God is presented metaphorically as the sword of the Spirit (Eph. 6:17). The more Word we have, the more we can stand against the enemy's wiles. Remember, it was the Word of God that our example – Jesus, used against the Devil and was victorious on every count.

*"For the word of God is quick, powerful, and sharper than any two-edged sword, piercing even to the dividing asunder of soul and spirit, and the joints and marrow, and is a discerner of the thoughts and intents of the heart." (Heb. 4:12)* The Word of God is essential to this whole warfare. It is the Word with which we resist the enemy of our souls.

The fellowship of the saints forms that earthly security that we all need. The Word of God declares: *"Not forsaking the assembling of ourselves together, as the manner of some is, but exhorting one another: and so much the more, as ye see the day approaching." (Hebrews 10:25)* *"Where no counsel is, the people fall: but in the multitude of counsellors there is safety." (Proverbs 11:25).* *"For by wise counsel thou shalt make thy war: and in a multitude of counsellors there is safety." (Proverbs 24:6)* *"Iron sharpeneth iron; so, a man sharpeneth the countenance of his friend." (Proverbs 27:17) "Then they that feared the LORD spake often one to another: and the LORD hearkened and heard it, and a book of remembrance was written before him for them that feared the LORD, and that thought upon his name." (Malachi 3:6).*

**Prayer Time**

Free at last indeed has been the longing of my heart, dear Father. Thank You for sending Your Son, Jesus Christ of Nazareth, for paying the ultimate price for my freedom. I embrace this victory and being made more than a conqueror through His work on the cross.

I rely not on my strength to maintain this victory, but I stand in the strength and power granted by Your Holy Spirit. Therefore, I suit myself in full armor, grasping the shield of faith and sword of the Spirit to defend the freedom grounds gained and doors closed through this process of deliverance and restoration.

Dear Father, help me to be bold in sharing my testimony to assist someone else in becoming free from the clutches of this diabolical enemy of our souls.

Amen!

# CHAPTER 11
# MOVING ON
# HOW CAN I STAY FREE?

As we conclude this writing, please use the list below for further information and instructions on keeping your freedom. It is possible!

Credit to Frank Marzullo for the following tips from the book *"Eight Keys to Spiritual and Physical Health."*

### How To Keep Your Freedom

1. Total commitment to Christ (Matthew 23:37, John 12:26)
2. Obey God instead of engaging in works to please Him (Hebrews 4:9-11)
3. Be accountable to someone to watch over your life (Hebrews 13:7,17; 1 Thessalonians 5:12)

4. Regularly study and draw life from the Word of God (Psalm 119:9, 105 & 165)
5. Put on and wear the armor of God, standing strong in the power of His might. (Ephesians. 6:10-18)
6. Pray in all circumstances: thanksgiving, praise, and worship. (1 Thessalonians 5:17, Psalm 100)
7. Keep in fellowship with spiritually minded people. (Hebrews 10:24-25)
8. Regularly make positive confessions of faith in God's ability and power, which is working in you. (Mark 11:22-24, Romans 10:8-10)
9. Remember all demons are powerless as you abide in Christ's victory. (Luke 10:19)
10. Do not be yoked to unbelievers (2 Corinthians 6:14-7:1)
11. Memorise and understand your position in Christ (Zechariah 3;1-3&7, Galatians 2:20)
12. Deal promptly with sin (Isaiah 59:2, 1 John 1:9)
13. Forgive and forget (Matthew 6:14-15, 17:1-2, 18:15-35, Hebrews 10:17)

14. Keep home life in order or restore it to divine order (1 Timothy 3:3- 15, Eph. 5:18-33; 6:1-4)
15. Submit yourself to God. (James 4:7)

The above list is not a repellent against future attacks or temptations from Satan and his horde of demons. Instead, they are keys or armories in your arsenal to resist Satan and his cohorts when they launch their attacks. Note: The keys are for resistance, not cessation-they will not stop Satan from planning, plotting, or scheming to destroy your life. However, like a flood, the Spirit of the Lord will lift a standard against him.

A total commitment to Christ is paramount; without this, the enemy can have a foothold in your life. Remember that disobedience establishes a curse, and demons carry out curses. Hence, it is vital to submit totally to God in obedience to His word, so having an accountability partner that would hold the mirror of the Word before you can save you from falling into the traps of the Devil.

There can never be an overemphasis on specific Christian disciplines, such as prayer, fasting, and studying the Word. Prayer strengthens your interpersonal relationship with God. Fasting puts the flesh under subjection, decreasing its appetites and cravings. Study of the Word encourages you to be who God has created you to be – victors, not victims.

In studying, meditating, and memorizing the scriptures, you will find yourself walking more and more in victory as the word comes alive in you. You begin to see everything through the lens of the Word and will have the proper perspective on each situation you face.

Apostle V. T. Williams always shares the story of four united bulls who were scouted for a meal by a lion. The lion knew that as long as the bulls were united, it could not defeat them. The lion then instinctively separated all four from each other. Eventually, the lion had its meal; subsequently, the lion had them as his meal one after the other. So, if we stand in a victory against the devil's wiles, we must stand united in fellowship. Forget not the assembling of ourselves together as iron sharpens iron.

Be not entangled again in the yoke of bondage but deal promptly with sin. Repent and renew your mind daily with the word of God. Circumcising every thought that does not bring glory to Christ, whilst speaking the Word of God daily over your life like multivitamins that build your spiritual immune system.

As you embark on a new phase in your life, remember that *"old things are passed away."* 2 *Corinthians 5:17: "Forget those things which are behind and reach for those that are ahead."* Philippians 3:13. Discipline is crucial in seeing a change in your life. So, put yourself under the strict order of the Word of God; you will find "eternal life" in them.

# CLOSING WORDS

Deliverance does not bring victory or transformation in life; it is a cleansing, and then success comes by allowing Christ to enter a person's life and take control of that life. To experience this transformation and victory, we must:

1. Confess our sins, renounce them, and ask Christ to cleanse us by His precious blood and become the Lord of our lives.
2. Forgive those who have hurt us. It must be genuine, releasing joy and freedom in our lives.
3. Ask those we have wronged to forgive us.
4. Renounce all works of Satan in which we were involved. Destroy any instruments that Satan involved us in, e.g., the Ouija board.
5. Read the Word of God daily.
6. Begin a consistent prayer life.

7. Find a good Christian church and submit to the leadership. (James 5:16)

Father, thank you for enabling me to make this material available to my brothers and sisters in the body. Grant us sustained victory over all the onslaught of the devil and his cohort of demons. Success is ours through the blood of the cross. We claim and operate by it in Jesus' name.

Amen!

# TESTIMONIES

In conclusion, I would like to share with you a few testimonies.

I remember being asked by one of the pastors of my church to minister to a lady who had called at the church asking for someone to come and pray with her but to administer deliverance to her first. The story was that her husband and she were having marital issues. He had three other women along with her. And all four of them were working witchcraft on her.

The demons assigned to her were having intercourse with her at night. These spirits were having both anal and vaginal sex. I remember Dr. Donald Stewart, Reverend Dwight Thompson, and I met with her one night at approximately 8 p.m. We began praying for her, and that session lasted until 4:00 AM. We watched as her body contorted in pain. She wailed loudly as the demons were exiting her body from both areas. After an experience such as that, I strongly recommend that once the session is with a female, be sure to have a female minister involved.

There was another situation that I recall. For this one, I had Rev. Leostone Morrison with me. This lady was hurt immensely by her husband. He was having an affair and brought the other woman into their home for their sexual escapades. She became bitter, angry, resentful, and unforgiving. She came to the church acknowledging her need for deliverance, but left without being completely free, as she chose to forgive others but refused to forgive her husband.

Rev. Morrison and I had taken her into a private room and began to administer deliverance to her. During our ministry, we recognized that she was harboring unforgiveness, blocking her freedom. The first person she forgave was her Pastor, as she thought he took too long to come and address the issue. She forgave others but could not muster the courage to forgive her husband.

When we had gotten to the point of her forgiving her husband, she said, "To forgive him was like forgiving satan." We stood by and watched her tummy grow to look like a woman pregnant for nine months. We continued praying for her and heard her having labour pains. We saw the headwater break. The Holy Spirit instructed that we should perform a mime of a cesarean section. At this juncture, we called for two ladies at work in the offices to come and assist. We informed them what the Spirit's instructions were and exited the room. Sometime later, when we inquired about her state, the ladies said she refused to forgive her husband and left with a large tummy and in pain. No one is worth your eternal soul but God.

My wife and I were invited to a church youth camp to minister. After sharing the word, we call for persons who need ministry to come forward. One beautiful young lady came forward, and when I began ministering to her, the demons in her became agitated. She started flashing her left hand. I noticed there was a ring on her finger. When I asked where she got the ring, she said it was her engagement ring.

She was engaged to be married later that year. I said something was wrong with this ring. I then asked her permission to remove it from her finger to which she consented. As we continued, she confessed that the mother of the young man she was to marry was involved in witchcraft and had "fixed" the ring. By "fixed", I mean it had witchcraft placed on it to make sure she got married to the son.

A pendant was also on her chain, half of a heart. The husband-to-be had the other half. Following the leading of the Holy Spirit, we removed both items, and you could hear the demons screaming from her approximately a mile away. She was free and had the spiritual fortitude to call off the wedding.

Rev. Morrison and I were called to the house by a mother deeply concerned about her son. She related that he got dressed one day and left the house. He got to the bus stop, returned home, changed his clothes, and went to bed. After that experience, he became a different person. He began using expletives uncontrollably and found it difficult to converse with.

In the process of ministering to him, he began speaking expletives. Someone tried to stop him because they thought he was offensive. I told them to leave him alone as the demons were becoming weakened. He went on for a bit longer but eventually stopped.

The Lord identified that the demons we were now to deal with came into him through a self-defense practice - karate. I started calling the karate ranks by their belts: green, brown, black, etc. While doing so, demons were screaming and leaving his body. To God be all the glory; he was entirely free that day.

Some years while serving as the Youth Pastor at the church, I am now a pastor. I was preparing for the youth fellowship when the office phone rang. It was approximately two hours past office closing time, and I was reluctant to answer. However, I got the nudge to answer. A young lady seeking prayer and ministry was on the other end. She was actually on the job.

I counselled her for around forty-five minutes, then began to pray. While praying, I heard a growling voice say, "She is mine, and I am not coming out." I became righteously indignant, addressed the spirit, and commanded it to leave her body immediately. There was a roar, and the line went dead.

I was astounded, as this was the first time I had done a deliverance session over the phone. After a few moments had passed, I heard her sobbing. Curiosity got the better of me, so I asked what just took place. The young lady said that when I was addressing the evil spirit, she felt the muscles in her tummy tighten as if something was trying to leave her body. She vomited, and there was slime on the floor.

She proceeded to ask me what all of the slime vomiting meant. I explained to her that the muscles tightened when the demons resisted - not wanting to leave. The vomiting was because demons carry mess with them; when they go, they take their garbage. I have never heard from this person again. It was a first for me. I trust she is still walking in victory.

Kirk, one of my main ministry partners, and I had a session with a young man who worked for him. He was being tormented in his sleep by demons having intercourse with him. As we prayed for him, I recall him saying the demons wanted to come out through his anus. We expelled those demons while he was passing some flatulence of a horrible odor. He then said he felt other evil spirits moving in his penis. We began to command those to leave. Within a few moments, he urinated on himself.

I was preaching at a crusade in Discovery Bay, St. Ann. I usually use Friday nights for deliverance, as most people would not work the next day, and this can be lengthy. After the proclamation of the word, I made an altar call for persons needing prayers for deliverance. Amongst those at the altar was a man whose tongue began to move back and forth out of his mouth like a snake.

Pointing to him, I said to the demon, "Get out of him, you serpentine spirit." He immediately fell to the floor. Lying on his back, he started slithering like a snake and headed toward the church's back door. I came off the rostrum, kicked off the right foot of the shoe, stepped on his chest (youthful exuberance), and made the declaration again. He shook his head, and he popped his eyes wide open.

He began looking around as if he were in a strange place. When he rose to his feet, he asked me what had happened. I explained to him. He said the last thing he remembered was when I started praying. What had taken place then was that the demon had taken control of him. He left the meeting that night, confessing to feeling lighter and free.

As a youngster, I worked with my spiritual father, Apostle V. T. Williams, in a crusade in the Duhaney Park area of Kingston, Jamaica. One evening at the altar, a young lady displayed signs of demonic manifestation. The confessions came that she was a dancer from a strip club in another part of the island. She also struggled with bisexuality. Through prayer, Apostle Williams and the team brought deliverance to her that night.

She went back to the previous lifestyle and became demonized again. Only this time, she was in a worse condition. As the bible records in Mat 12:43-45: "When an evil spirit comes out of a person, it travels through dry places looking for a place to rest, but it finds none. So, it says, *"I will go back to the home I left.' When it comes back, it finds that the home is still empty. It is all neat and clean. Then the evil spirit goes out and brings seven other spirits more evil than itself. They all go and live there, and that person has even more trouble than before. It is the same way with the evil people who live today."* (ERV)

I was doing what had become the norm at this time. After the morning services on a Sunday, I would stay at church for two reasons: 1. It was too far to go home and return for the evening service, and 2. I enjoyed praying in the sanctuary. So, there I was with my routine when I saw this young lady walking into the sanctuary. I noticed that something was wrong. I started a conversation with her that confirmed my suspicions.

There was an elder who lived nearby, so I went and called him. On my return, one of the church mothers was on the premises. We all ministered to her in the prayer room. While carrying her through the process, one of the demons said, "If you want me to leave, go for seven other persons whose names start with 'R', and I will leave. Right then, the Holy Spirit brought the above text to mind.

We did not grant that request and cast them all out. I am delighted to say that the last time I made contact with this young lady, she had graduated from Bible School and was an ordained minister in her church. Hallelujah!!!! We are delivered to deliver others.

God has called the members of His body to proclaim His word to the captives and bring deliverance to those bound by demons. We must equip ourselves and make no more excuses. The church has been quiet for too long, allowing the devil to rampage through this world and even the church. Deliverance ministry is not for some "Special Operations Team" but for every disciple of Jesus Christ.

***HE IS COMING FOR A GLORIOUS CHURCH!***

# ABOUT THE AUTHOR

David Grant has been a Christian since the age of 11 and has been involved in deliverance ministry since 16. He has lectured on Evangelism, Demonology, and Deliverance. David serves as Pastor at The Jamaica Evangelistic Centre and is also the Founder of Odigia Global, a personal and leadership development organization. At present, he is pursuing a master's degree in executive Christian Leadership.

He is married to Juliet, and they have four adult children, two sets of twins: Joel and Danielle, Jhenelle and Jhonelle. David and Juliet also serve the body of Christ as relationship counsellors and coaches.

Made in the USA
Middletown, DE
09 December 2025

22440506R00071